for when she's feeling blue

poetry by
edgar holmes

1

also by edgar holmes:

her favorite color was yellow

my love,

in my first book, i wrote
about how much i loved you.

in my second book, i am
writing you messages of hope
and inspiration for when
you're feeling blue. i hope
that you will always remember
them when you need them most.

edgar

CHAPTERS

Chapter One

Blue

i know that nothing
can cure
the sadness
embedded deep within
your heart

but love
can crack open your shell
and let in the light

my love, i will always be here
when you need me most
to love you
and hold you close

i know that sometimes
you feel
as if the world
is collapsing
on top of your head

but do not lose hope
because i know you

and i know that you
are strong enough
to hold up the chaos
and find your peace
even when it seems
impossible

i hate their ignorant
statements
the way they tell you
to stop worrying
or think positive thoughts
as if such trite quips
could suddenly cure
the chemical imbalance
in your brain

if only depression
  was that simple

i wish that i was able
to take the burden
off your shoulders

and though i cannot voyage
into your mind
and help you carry
your sadness and fear

know that i
am right here beside you
through it all

you taught me that pain
is not something to hide,

that scars shouldn't be hidden
under long sleeved shirts

i wish that my love for you
could overflow these pages
and inscribe itself
permanently
onto your skin
so that you never forget
you are

l o v e d

you cannot help
but compare yourself
to everyone else

but know this, my love
there is no one on earth
who compares to you
in any way

you are my definition
of perfect

i love the way
your eyes look
as i wake up next to you
in the morning

sleepy, content,
so effortlessly beautiful

your insecurities
creep up on you
and tell you
you are not enough

but you are

do not forget that

as long
as i have you
to wake up to

everything
will be
just fine

don't be afraid
to take some time
to take care
of yourself

self care
is the easiest thing
to forget

you ask me if you are too much
to handle. my darling, i would
light the world on fire just
to dance in the flames with
you.

i will never let you go
no matter how hard
things get

i will always hold you close
feel your heartbeat
against mine

i have always been afraid
of growing old

but now
having loved you
i now see that i was afraid
of the wrong thing

i'm not afraid of growing old

i'm afraid of growing old,
knowing that i lost a love as
powerful as ours, the only
thing that made life
meaningful.

it is okay
to admit
that you are broken

we cannot all be strong
all the time

it is okay
to take the time
to piece yourself
back together

mistakes
when turned into lessons
are not mistakes
at all

all that matters
is that we learn
as we live on

do not be
too hard
on yourself

dear god,

show me how
to take the happiness she
gives me
and give it back to her

i know that you shy away
when i take pictures
of you

but know that i will cherish
each and every one
of these sacred memories
as we look back
on a life well lived
together

her soul
is a patch of soil

what you plant there
she will grow

so place where you can
seeds of lovely roses

compliments and hope and
affirmation

and watch her bloom

love grows the most
beautifully
for those who have the
patience
to take care of it
tenderly

the angels dance
at your laughter
and heaven shines down
when you smile

if i could only be
a mirror
for the light she is
in my life

i could light
the whole world
with her love

the greatest gift
life gave me

was spending time
with you

i want to love you
better
than anyone else
has ever loved you
before

i shudder to think
that in another life
i had to live
without you

you
are a field of sunflowers
in human form

when you're feeling blue
know that there
is nothing that i
wouldn't do for you

x

Chapter Two

Night

when the night seems
to stretch on forever
and it feels like hope
will never come over
the horizon
again

know that dawn always comes
and hope
will return to you
in due time

nothing could have prepared me
for the tremendous sadness
of thinking
i had lost you

i knew it was true love
when i couldn't stop
loving you
not just in the good times
but when things were hard

the night is long
and hope may feel lost
but do not forget
that there is always
a silver lining

the thing about the night
is it's the only time
you can see the stars

a thousand nights
in bed together

and yet
every night
it always feels
as if there is something new
to try

men:

take all of the energy
you waste
on checking out other girls
and liking their photos
on instagram

and use it
on your woman
to show her
how much you desire her

never let her feel
unwanted

we are invincible
as long as we
tell each other
the truth

a relationship built on trust
is strong enough
to withstand
the winds of petty jealousies

i wish that every time
you looked in the mirror
you saw the same perfection
that i see
every day

you have made it through
tough times before

do not let
the difficulties ahead
make you forget
how far
you have already come

the world is too vast
and dense
to leave a legacy

i know that i will be
forgotten
soon after i die
no matter how much i try
to fight against
that fact

but as long as i know
i made your life
better

that will be enough
for me

though i think you are perfect
know that this is not because
i put you
on some pedestal

i don't think you're perfect
because you have no flaws

i think you're perfect
because you live your life
with such beautiful freedom
unafraid
of being seen
for who you truly are

one of the many ways
i know i love you
is because of small silly
things
like the times
i've cheated at games
to let myself lose
and let you win

i just love to see your joy
at small little things

and i'd rather see you happy
than just try to win

i don't care
if there is no more purpose
to my life
than loving you

that is more than enough
for me

your love
softened my hard edges
and sewed up
the wounds
of past heartbreaks

i always thought
that i
wasn't tough enough
and that no girl
would ever love me
because i was not
'manly' enough

but you loved me
for who i am
without caring
about silly things
like that

i only hope
i can show you
the same
unconditional love

let's sneak out
onto the roof
just like old times
with some rose petals
and a bottle of wine

let's look at the stars
and admire the sky
let me tell you i love you
as i look in your eyes

i know there will be
good days
and bad days

i think
it's almost more important
to show you i love you
on the bad days
than it is
on the good days

there's something about
persevering
even when it isn't easy

though i love
to admire you
with my eyes

i also love
to admire you
with my hands
lips
and tongue
in the darkness

don't let
their unkind words
get to you

they are just jealous
of your effortless goodness

i will rub the stress
out of your shoulders
until you are sound asleep
then tuck you into bed
with a glass of water
by your bedside table

when you've found someone
who lights your heart
on fire

what's the use
in waiting
or holding back?

i want to spoil you
in every way
possible

x

Chapter Three

Hope

hope
does not exist
without despair
for if it did
it would have no meaning

realize that in the same way
your triumph
over your struggles
will be all the more powerful
because of the struggle
you went through

it doesn't have to be
elaborate
but spending time
with your partner
is so important

just taking a walk
or having a picnic

don't forget
to spend time together

people love each other
in different ways

a lot of pain can be avoided
by communicating
how you want to be loved
and how your partner
wants to be loved

treat your relationship
like it's important
and put in the work
to make it last

yin and yang
your body
and mine

harmony
reflection
symmetry

so this is what it feels like
to be all in on someone

no safety nets, no second
options

my love, i am absolutely
committed
to you

you look at the path ahead
and see
that you have
so much further
to go

but i want you to realize
that every inch is a victory
and you can be proud of
yourself
to have made it this far

know this:

i will always be there
arms wide open
ready
to catch you
when you fall

you
are the reason
the sun shines
in the morning

as long
as you keep
holding on
to your hope
that things
will get better

then nothing
can truly
stop you

arguments happen
even between the best of
couples

the important thing is
to stay determined
to move past it
and mend
what has been broken

sometimes it feels
like there could never be
a remedy
for your broken heart

but do not forget
that even the worst of wounds
heal
if given enough time

you can't escape your troubles
in a bottle of whiskey

you may be able
to push them
below the surface
for the night

but they will always
come back to the surface
in the morning

who needs getting high
when i have you

you make me feel
high
all the time

fate did not
bring us together
across vast distances
and through many tribulations

just to let us fall apart
when we need each other
most

the only thing
more important
than having nothing
to hide

is being with someone
who trusts you enough
to not check
if you do

you make me feel

w h o l e

in ways
no one else
ever did
before

i wish i could fall in love
with life
half as well
as you do

do not forget
more than anything else
that we are just human

reach out
with open arms
and a forgiving heart

hope
is my hand
in yours

you
in my arms

me
telling you
everything
is going
to be
alright

do not forget
what made you
fall in love
in the first place

she was the lightning
shooting across the sky
not afraid
to make her mark
on the world

never forget
that before
you are anyone else's

you

are

your

own

i can't make
your sorrow
disappear

but i can hold you
and make you forget them
at least for a moment

x

Chapter Four

Light

winter
never lasts
forever

her love was an ocean
and i
was just learning
to swim

learning to be happy
is such a painful, long
process

sometimes it feels
like the journey
will never
bring you
anywhere

i never want
the sun to set
on an argument
between us

no matter
how angry we are
with each other

we have to be committed
to starting fresh
with each morning

i think people like the idea
of love
as something that solves
all your problems

it isn't
and that's okay

romance is not
for the impatient
or lazy

romance takes patience
and hard work

if you are not willing
to build
towards the stars

do not bother
laying a foundation
in the first place

the hardest days are when you
have to put on a mask of
happiness for the sake of
those around you, but you
realize by keeping them safe
from worry you are only
isolating yourself from their
helping hands

strength
does not come
from hardening your heart
so much
that nothing
can harm it

strength
comes from the ability
to be hurt
and still be vulnerable
still willing
to risk pain
for the sake of love

do not be afraid
to let go of people
who constantly
bring a cloud
of negativity
in front
of your sun

happiness
that has been fought for
and taken
from the jaws
of despair
is so much more meaningful
than easy happiness
which flows effortlessly
from a good life

you may think
that your struggle
and your scars
make you weak

but your struggle
is what will make you
strong enough
to get through anything
life can throw at you

i am convinced that there is
not one thing that we could
not accomplish, as long as we
do it together

i swear, my darling
the way you love me
is enough to make me
believe
in
m a g i c

i never want you to feel
any doubt
about whether or not
i am here for you

if it takes
every second
of every day
i will give you
all the evidence
you could ever want
of my devotion to you

i think there is something
beautiful about the way we had
to struggle and work for what
we have instead of having it
handed to us

never let your life become so
busy that you do not have time
for the only person who truly
matters

you taught me to live my life
fearlessly

to be excited
about the possibilities
for good things

instead of terrified
of the things
that could go wrong

more than anything
i just want you
to know

that knowing you
has made me
a better person

my darling
no matter where
we are

you always make me feel
at home

i feel so lucky
that i get
to make new memories
with you

rather than look through
our pictures
and wonder
what might have been

i want to be the one
who is always there for you
even when you feel
completely alone

you taught me that sometimes
the most beautiful roses grow
from the cracks in the
concrete and not just in
gardens

if nothing else
remember that you
are strong enough
to face your struggles
even when it feels
like you can't
keep
holding on

you can do this.

i promise.

to my readers,

thank you so much for
supporting my work and
allowing me to keep writing
about the only person who
makes my life feel like it
matters.

if you don't already know, my
first book is called 'her
favorite color was yellow'.
but i'm guessing if you're
reading this you already knew
that.

anyway, thank you and i love
you all. if you want to reach
out to me, you can reach me at
edgarholmesauthor@gmail.com.

thank you.

-edgar holmes

Made in the USA
Columbia, SC
02 December 2019

84239248R00071